AF227960

LINGHEART
PUBLISHING

CHANGE

LINGHEART PUBLISHING

Lingheart Publishing preserves and experiments with different forms and perspectives in English language and literature. It furthers this objective to enlighten readers by exploring subjects that are a crucial part of the millennium age.

Published in the United Kingdom by Lingheart Publishing, Portsmouth.

Lingheart speciesism edition published in October 2018 (Lingheart Publishing).

Contents

Dream

Humans looked up for the first time.

They felt scarred and tainted deep.

She wondered if looking inside

would show them underneath.

He shied away for a moment to instil,

wondering whether it was okay to look,

wondering whether unknown was real.

She looked up this time but felt shook.

Closer now holding onto one another,

he wondered if this unknown was real.

She opened her mouth, but words were.

The words were not yet there to reveal.

Language had lost them somewhere.

He stared a blank that told no despair,

looking for someone they could trust,

not finding someone but everything us.

Everything? They thought. It cannot be

We do not deserve everything. Solely

from the future, she looked away. Fear

in a tear formed in her eye sincere.

Seeing through the watery plural pupils,

and deep inside life at an eternal light…

but we do not have light? They thought.

He looked away. Standing still for time,

she could not move if she were to try.

They held one another and it felt safe.

But we are not safe? They thought.

They looked around foreseeing a knife.

But only found one inside of their head

holding it was a dark energy of rights.

Please let us go now, they said.

But no words were formed transformed.

No words could bear their soul endured.

His physical body was a heavy condition,

too heavy for his gentle hearts' revision.

A crumpled flower was now a fragile art,

unwilling to part she fainted from thought

that she would now have to create talk.

Embracing one another and one far light

when we do not have light, they thought.

Wake up my dear love. He opened now

his eyes for the first time in years, torn.

She whispered; her gentle lips so fragile.

He wondered why they were. She looked

up. So pure, so strong, he thought. Shook.

It was only a dream. Sobbing in your sleep

at night. My love, you have always wept.

You have always been here. You have always

been one. I whisper it every night to you. Stay

while you fall asleep and cry. But why am I part…

not with you, she thought. But then his heart

said, you are not with yourself right now. Neither

am I my love? Wait for love to revive you deeper,

my love. And in all time, we will never be apart.

She looked down at her heart,

and it was now one glow, I will send my soul

to you soon to show you will go on a journey.

When your body arrives, I want your whole

spirit inside. And I will come and bring we…

you back. I will bring you back to life,

my love. Just remember what I said.

You are the universe shining bright.

And you will shine. Now be present,

you will form one heart.

Now take your eyes

off this nightmare start.

Let collective love rise.

Recollection
The embodiment of all of human dashes

lets the crosses come out as circles

to entice singularity. Humans believing ashes

of truths that are not true. Humans are full

believing in an incompleteness. Exist.

The incompleteness lay underneath

human mask. Look for the self. Witness

the bearings of the soul. Self leaves

it open and closed as it is sent through

the mind. The pulling pulls self toward.

It pulls self toward the one that is within

Reach, in the moment. Gripped forward

by a false concept of a moment in time,

human is subject to the figure that it holds.

These are subjective figures that it moulds,

that appear diverse in what human entwine.

But it is forward nature intrinsically similar

to a backward nature. Humans cannot decipher.
Humans decipher these dashes, with hindsight
a humans' logical brain will fire lines that bite.

Lines travel through this existence putting in
place crosses. Beings are putting everything
together. They are giving humanity the dashes
that they encounter to form their brain flashes.

Their brain programs itself based on an interlude
of moments that they should question. Underly.
The beautiful lie is everything. The ugly inside
truth is the bearing of their soul. The ugly truth

inside the bearings of their soul. They open
their self up to bear witness. Humans feel witness.
The backwards morality. Humans feel it come
through them in abrupt clearness. The clearness

looks into their brain and makes them challenge
their self. They challenge each fibre abstraction
that once held a dash. They hold onto these dashes

and weep. They weep like they have never for masses.

They seek answers to each and every one of collective.

Everything will tell them everything. They will see

the ugly truth through the beauty that truth intends

to bestow upon who they really are. They are free.

They are free in a way that their brain could not fathom

before. They are the comparison to what once was.

They are the comparison to what now is, to what seldom

always was, and to what will permanently remain.

The crosses and dashes will always stay the same.

But they can now look forward and move forward

because they have found their bearings and changed.

They have found a collective soul and will undo the chains.

Amethyst
Looking at this empty world,

inside was an amethyst heart

full of these broken promises.

Looking at this empty word,

now this polluted piece existing

both meaningless and absent.

Reminiscent of the human lost…

lost in their own brief absence.

Thinking of the self existing alone

only taking time to suit their own

in their blind thoughts. Postponed

thinking about their life, absent

life uncompromised and yet foretold

not going through to what is beyond.

At their best the world has meaning.

Their best the worlds' worst feeling,

they do not see the worlds' pain

through acknowledgment alone.
But, when it is time to feel life again,
when it is time to feel action hone,

they go back and they postpone.
But still conceiving they are earthly,
the thought is connivingly unearthly.
They do not do or begin the unknown.

They think they do but it is stages.
Books still did not educate the self,
but are still deep and full of pages.
They are as deep as empty shelf…

shelf brain seeped with the pollution.
They mean something unaware here
all the while giving nothing of solution
looking at this empty world as sincere.

This blank space humans could fill
was the world at surface level still.
Humans thinking, they had all to give

but nothing much else and all to resist.

If they look inside the world at nothing,

the heart has inscribed words buffering.

These words were always absent still

but now even more so gone from will.

The heart inside began to say this intact:

"There is no set path,

Just follow your heart."

As long as their path does not impact

the heart, intact. Do think of the world…

deeper world beyond the existing self.

Conditioned to think of importance, bold.

But behind that thought is something else.

In time, they will expand the existing self

beyond the thought of everything else.

The world is more than a polluted piece…

a polluted piece with places and deceit.

Write the world and write empty words.

The empty words from a mind as bleak

as this compromised and defective heart.

The worlds' life is an amethyst heart.

Change

Path

Dragging my feet along on a stony and damp path.

Those before me were a pile of tragic, unspoken deceits,

looking at the bleak buildings that would soon depart.

Only seeing the stones as one wall as no cracks seep,

I drag my feet along. I drag my self along. I drag. I drag.

The sun went down and the winds blew up each snag.

There was a sense of loss but a map that remained hidden…

remaining hidden from the ones that went where forbidden.

I drag. I drag. The path below but a wet mess of water.

Water and mud. Lumpy and old with past stories for-told.

I dragged my feet through it and felt it reach my ankle,

like a chain that pretended to be open instead of shackle.

Please stop. Please. I sobbed to my self in the pitch black.

I could only when the dark was in a place of complete lack.

Invisible now, as the weeps from within began to crack…

crack open on the outside of my eyes of which were back.

I opened them now and saw a path ahead from my pain

Change

from which a new world and love awaited in my shame.

The path reached a point where I had to begin to swim.

I stared at the mud for a second until I decided to dive in.

Covered now in a consuming liquid that was heavy to bear,

I moved, because I saw the future as if it was already there.

I could not breath and I could not see with my eyes open.

I had to go within my self and feel the words yet unspoken.

I pulled my self out of the mud and collapsed onto green.

My favourite colour now surrounded by as glass gleamed.

I was merely watching my self from a screen existent above.

I was not dirty. I was untouched.

Observing footage was enough.

Change

Sea

Fish surrendered on a rock in the middle of the sea.

The water had ripples and remained in motion

still, as the words they felt were far underneath.

Still moving their eyes to look at loves' devotion,

beyond the water words stayed. The fish were withdrawn.

Many storms had come and left them weak and worn.

Their eyes were still wet when the weather was now dry

after being on the rubble as all the years went by.

The rain that fell seemed to last a thousand years.

Nowhere from there. The damp on their skin smeared.

This sensation exemplified as suffering prolonged

because as the wind blew through the air felt ice cold.

But the fish were just wet on their body's surface somehow.

If they were cold inside, they would sure be dead by now.

They would have died from the cold and be swept far out.

Somehow inside, their heart still bared warmth from without.

Even though this rock was cold, and their homes torn,

they had not eaten anything in years but did not mourn.

And when the night fell lack of sight awakened fears.

The world sat with them on its knees exhausting tears

far too long as wet rippled, like the deep water that swayed

at times. The world would curl in a ball and disappear far away

inside itself… away from the ocean of words that would persist.

Fish could not see it as they curled on the rocks rocky surface.

But when the world got back up the water was to exhaust again

with the words beneath the ocean. Fish could not see anything

too far beneath and away to give them any true feeling of clarity.

This was a time where the world would envision love to clear disparity.

Change

Lost

It drags its feet along the floor

and picks up the dust ignored.

It chose to live with no one life

choosing to be some of one write

as wrong, as it felt to only hide

in a room that made mind feel.

At heart, it wanted to slowly die

as it lost sight of what was real.

It wrote things that it inside knew

would not give audience appeal.

But it is what was now necessary

through words unknown in away.

Dragging its feet along every day,

along the desk and all the decay

it felt its life was intrinsic wasting.

It managed to type on something.

Something of thousands of projects,

it had already seen in its world head.

But choosing the most bad one first

knowing its heart was full of neglect,

the words were not the term best.

But it tried to describe those dead

as it hurtfully put aside the rest

in its pathetic and blank order bed.

Sitting there with eyes dulled down

with delusions of life, and an ill frown

looking at the trash beside its soul

as if it were now its hearts' one soul.

Maybe it would write when it could.

Because in its heart was all.

In its thought, all it could see…

All it could see creative, in some way

still, as days grew old and dulled away.

It had no means to life,

or a language known.

It had no form of right.

It was a being all alone.

Change

Self

I am embracing the unique source of expression that I am. I understand my feelings. I am understood by those around me. I see my self... as self... through my unique expression and connection with the universe. Oneness. We are all one.

Through acknowledging and accepting how I feel, I am also becoming more in align with what is. Because I am an intrinsic part of the universe. We are all one.

We are all part of all else that is. I am in alignment with oneness because I define who I am and my sense of self. My authentic self is connected to everything else that exists. I accept my self. I can express how I feel without being afraid because I am in alignment with everything else that exists. I am one with the universe. I am able to decide what actions I can take moving forward that will be an expression of who I am. My personal truth. Self-expression. I can be my self. I know how I feel. I admit how I feel. I express how I feel. I am finding my self every single day. At all times, because time is a path we use in order to comprehend something much greater. We are one.

Change

Subliminal

The world in this today

is not what it should be.

It is but a void in space

with all suffering seas.

The world in this today

intuition can make better.

Feel to have the intention

to build a home forever.

The world in this today

is not what it should be.

One will object hatred

and long for all equality.

The world in this today

weighs on true hearts.

You should see it now

as a once fragile place

that forever holds all us.

The world before today

all relied on too heavily

with no real reciprocity.

All use free resources.

All build from no veins

in time where creation

came in a state of vain.

The world in this today

made humanity a true

self. The world in today

made every being you.

The inhabitants here,

here in this one world,

were made from this.

The places we killed.

The world today

should be equal,

should be all just,

should feel right.

And think about the now.
And all the times you say
goodnight.   Goodnight.

Goodnight world today.
I will strive for the place
of love for all of beings.

I will strive to remain awake
with wide eyes open seeing
that equality is all everything,
and the world is our all home
even in times of complication.
We are one and never alone.

Change

Figure

The marks on the figure are human somehow.

Humans take hold of world life and leave now.

Leave marks on the worlds' fragile figure behind.

Fingerprint marks will stain the collective mind.

The figure looks down at the translucent lies

and sees them almost gone, stained and bare.

Down down down at soft creation of demise.

Wet with teardrops. Humankind does not care.

Darkness over existence keeps light within

while closing figurative eyes to imagine when.

Still there. The torturous can only pretend.

Still there. Keep closing the world will mend.

The figure looks down as marks are conceived.

Marked upon it like a biological imprint. Leave.

Leave the world alone. Leave the world alone.

Please. Collective mind screams at humans

softly.

                              Change

The tears run while the figure stays still

and marks blend together without its will.

How then does the world move forward?

Fingerprint bruises.

How does the world turn back the time?

Bruises fingerprint.

Humans do not like having the power to mark.

Humans do not watch over figures in the dark.

But these purple, black, blue, brown, and grey

slowly began there fade away upon each day.

And each day the figure would take more steps.

Steps upon steps. Recovering forgiveness wept.

The figure and soul cleared through every being.

Humans could now penetrate deep within seeing.

Air

Evaporate the world and let it into human senses.

Stroke the nature until it becomes abstract undone.

Linger in collective consciousness as air caresses

with streams of thoughts that are almost finely one.

Scribble all over the world on expansive fine texture

onto stretched out landscape covered in scripture.

Pin it to the trees and turn it upside down to be one.

Leave the world there with life in a time that is undone.

Do not stop scribbling until the world sees the truth.

Do not stop the movement until the ground sees proof.

Extract what the world sees in creation. Extract truth.

If one can choose while putting it back together to undo,

know not what creation does know and know nothing

at all. Let life go into the depths of times that are fluid.

Fluids are absorbed into the world rather than rooted.

Let space become spaceless and curve human stroking.

Colours. Piece by piece all streams of thought together

converge in wonderless essence that needs no strands

of thoughts. Essence that needs no hands upon hands

hold not a means but a surrender of human existence.

Change

System

Human tears burrow away inside this one world

while other inhabitants stay in the same position

losing the collective mind through self-exclusion.

One world waits for humankind to make incision.

There is waste under oppressed feet and bars

between lips. Other inhabitants cannot move

and neither can those humans. Cold and hard

and damp. The wounds inside collective who

are left open other inhabitants weep loudly.

Humans loudly weep. Together weep loudly.

All loudly weep for… together weep loudly for…

love unconditional. All weep words. Forming

scars as they trickle down humankind,

these words would not stop dripping.

These words would not stop rubbing.

They are now a systematic infection.

These organs must all fulfil a function.

Words flow through the entire organism

and up to paths of energy in the brain.

Please know that humans will cleanse

and the world will be able to do the same.

Express all life. Express the world system.

It is not functional to not express repress.

One-self. One is expression. Oneness.

External and the internal. Oneness resists.

External and the internal expression persist.

External and internal form one collective,

heart.

Place
The world made me scream

in panic, I screamed for my life

expressing words that came.

The words came out of fright.

I screamed because I thought

in seconds I was going to die,

in a moment that was forced.

Forcing a world to decide upon my life,

the world shaped me from this place.

I am scared of going to any place now.

Place was another word for torture

as the world dragged me across

the floor, waiting with the knifes,

throwing things at me, pushing…

pushing me against the wall,

suffocating me until I then ignored.

But still with the world there inside

I… I tried to end my life many times.

I tried and I tried, and I tried

to escape the only torment.

I walked away many times.

But I realised somewhere

that no matter what I did

I was never going to be enough.

I looked down at my feet.

I looked down at nothing.

Everything I had was the worlds'

including my suffering.

I still hear those screams.

I still hear those screams.

I do not believe they are my own.

Change

Echo

Enlightenment moves each word.

Each word has traceable echoes

from one human to all the worlds

in an interpretable self-crescendo.

The minds of the humans grow

as these expansive waves flow

before opening collective self

and history completing it-self.

Words start hollowing. Combining

fluid waves of imperceptible limbo,

words begin to grow. Multiplying

and spiralling out into no vertigo,

the world uses words to express

an idea that is endless. No less.

Endless and expansive. No less.

Endless in the world. Yes. Endless.

The curves of energy in words tell

the story of every conditioned time.

Each curve foretells life line by line.

Time after time no-self hears all.

Every-one listens. One listens.

But humans do not hear words.

They do not feel these rewriting.

Do not feel their self-perception.

They do not see their interpretation

as the world shares the infinite words.

Words can and will rewrite all of one

of the one self. Words will all rewrite

all of their stories. Words will rewrite

human life. Each curve of the history

transmitting through history persists

until reaching humans' invisible lips.

Change

Star

Something magical, something beautiful,

came down from the glowing stars above

to guide us up to its level. One high enough.

We are drawn towards energy by the divine.

This intense sense of purpose we try to define.

We cannot define it still for it is far too immense.

The love we feel for all transcends as stars align…

transcends through time in an everlasting sense.

We come into union with much purpose unknown

to create a life together that is real and nature's own.

From the earth, to the stars, we have always loved all.

We continue to all still through a forever life fall,

the forever fall, which is the world that turns still.

The forever divine wheel that transforms our oath

on our souls' journey together moving growth.

This energy we cannot comprehend but feel.

Too much to conceal, but still itself concealing

the deep depths of life that are not yet revealing.

We can discover together through many lives

this destined path through the universe and times.

Name

Open the world up right now and take in every part of it.

Cut off all the sections and line them up in fluid symmetry.

Give them all names and place them in human category.

Put on a date and time for the sake of resistant expiratory.

Little do humans know that the faintest floods flush through.

The inhabitants here are laid down in layers of invisible blood

and given the right opportunity the world would give one love

and it would rotate free from human harm… breakthrough.

Forget all the hows and the ways that humans did resist.

The world does not need a reason to forgive or dismiss.

The world will forgive because humans are loving beings,

but that does not mean the suffering will be overseeing.

The world will look into humans and it will see unconditional light

when humans gave the world darkness at every backward desire.

Change what humans did throughout history as an innocent liar

into the unconditional collective future one can rise and admire.

Home

Love and light radiates through our world

and finds its way to transcend each way

into an abundance and expression overflow.

It flows into each challenge and each blessing

making its way by creating time and place

unchanging with each memory and aspiration

brightening every crevice and open space.

The past and the future make their indentation.

Painting the world with each and every kind of colour

unravelling up to the sky stem by stem as leaves show

into blossoming flowers new for more than days or hours

becoming a representation of every inspiration to grow.

Each picture on the surface tells a thousand stories.

Each space in between the lines shares

the words.

Each being that walks through creates their meaning.

Each emotion stays as the flowers continue sealing.

Sealing in the light that feeds their evergreen stem

so that even in times of   they will

not bend

for they gracefully   until the light comes back again

and when it does they will already be there

glowing

Falling
Completely insane imagining oppression

imagining the lunacy oppression would give

losing the plot and twirling into oppression

twirling and spiralling into unrealisation.

The hole of not understanding anything

was above as all beings endlessly fell.

Falling. Falling. Falling. Beings never fell

because in this oppressive state of being

one cannot fall if they are already falling.

Can one fall if they follow their higher self

down that hole. Self did not exist for years

in what oppression called the abyss of mental.

Mentalism. The ism of believing everything,

everything about what should not be

everything, that is not meant to happen

not existing in the right way with anything.

Bringing irrational behaviour to a halt

as it stops before self. Refusing to move

unable to comprehend anything around.

Fixing one-self by breaking, breaking open.

Smashing one-self onto the floor and scattering.

Jumping on ones' own broken fragments over

and over and over and over and over and over

until nothing is left but fragments of collective.

Serious

Waking up to oppression is a hollow space.

The lost potential came and went in disgrace.

Neglecting honest thoughts and staying in vain

with a being not aligned with the world in pain.

The plainest consumed the brink of every mind;

creativity would shrink; thoughts would unwind.

Thoughts not from one soul, or sadness within.

Thoughts of resentment and sweet bickering.

Time goes by while conditioning takes them—

The world can only wait for it to end.

Evolution exists for connections such as this.

Beings find themselves stuck feeling worthless.

Evolution should be taken seriously with grace.

Oppression transfuses blood with a new upgrade.

The commitment aligns every being into one.

There should be no time to think of dissection.

Waking up to oppression in a disconnected space:

the hollow space, not evolved, nor out of place

The steps toward evolution are serious ones

that wait for connections like this to become one.

Seasons
Autumn leaves were always falling.

They were dripping off the branches.

Drip by drip, they were always calling

to the winds. Not many could land

on the floor beneath their existence.

They just flew away with one another.

They flew past each park and fence

until once again reaching the summer

where trees had revived once again.

Trees would grow each and every year.

They stood firm when no leaves remain.

Wind would blow. And they would flow

still moving with the days and seasons.

And the weather, beings, and reasons

would still be there each and every day.

Trees may have only had their branches

but that was no sign that they had departed.

They stood firm when leaves were scattered everywhere.

Their roots imprinted on the ground to share

their intricacy with the world and all beings

in every situation without permanent leaving.

Mirrors

My mirror does not have a reflection.

There are marks and dirty fingerprints.

There are unforgiving people inside

of it. They say that I am faulty.

I am unacceptable. I stare at it

and in the dust that covers it.

I see words. Words are deforming it.

I should have taken better care of it.

Days pass and nothing changes.

Weeks and months pass, nothing changes.

I am nothing. I have no reflection.

I stare at the mirror and I feel rejection.

Not seen, I am a waste of space.

Or perhaps, I am a space full of waste.

If it saw my reflection, would it break?

Superstition says seven years bad luck.

The mirror says you are the bad luck.

I gather my thoughts in the dust.

Thoughts are in my brain, in my self,

and in my body. They are deformed.

Lucent
Waiting in a cell in a lonely community.

People see the weeps of this lonely solace

as erratic behaviour, waiting, longing,

weeping slowly on the cement wall.

Lucent. Stained with words and scribbles,

the tears run down the wall and turn black.

Not from ink tear that cannot be removed,

but painted over once every few years

from dust that has gathered in neglect.

They call for help but know what is next.

Words do not seem to form, nor release

from the mouth, but maybe from the neck.

If they could speak it would not matter,

the industry has invisible duct tape.

Nothing to see hear, they say together.

Nothing to see hear, already scripted.

But hear and you will see what is here.

End

Narrator: "Only functioning through humanity,

this infection has the world through to the end."

World: "I will be weak to the bone soon I admit.

You are the reason I am alive and I try to persist.

I have no idea how I survive. I stay only for you.

The love you give drip by drip is all that I value...

is all I need in order to exist till the end of time."

Infection: "Every sense is immensely heightened

when I am here inside my self alone. In my end,

I watch the days go by while here inside alone.

And I think about you as my only dearest home."

Wait
The world waits in torment.

Because it knows the truth

of delicate hands and will,

the world waits in torment.

Unable to keep itself still,

the world waits in torment.

Deteriorating in each day,

One will be a cure, dismay.

One will be a cure. Dismay.

The world waits in torment

with so much love to give.

Waiting to find self-worth

through life's duty of love,

the world waits in torment.

Is it not worth nothing more

than the torture that life is.

Will the world be able to forgive

those that are all broken.

Where is the Love?

Unspoken.

Sculpture
The sculpture began to crack.

Someone put the pieces back.

Stick them together with glue,

at least then it will be of value.

The sculpture began to crack.

Now its beauty is based on lack.

No one will buy it like this.

Now it is broken, is it worthless?

When it will not make a sale

their heart becomes stale.

There is nothing left to appreciate

Now that its figures depreciate.

There is no room for it in the hallway

gathering dust until it is thrown away.

Now it is a waste of space

sitting there ready to be replaced.

River

Orpheus, please save humanity

from this full river that overflows.

We are taken by strong current,

and all our previous deep woes.

Human life is the current ahead:

the path of those already dead.

Their body is bitten by all regret,

poisoned. Polluted venom sheds

through the tears upon tears, red.

The invisible tears you never see

are only made visible in reprieve.

In your loyal and plural murders,

along we flow now together

waiting to reach all the Gods,

who will awaken us this once

to a life. Eternal commitment

hand in hand, against all odds.

Change

Verb
These verbs manipulate

the concept of fluid time.

The verbs that translate

are called doing words.

Constantly shifted

in a back and forth,

the nouns that are

suppose to connect

never quite match.

Those doing words

overtake the nouns

and represent how

beings are transcending past

a phase of inward oppression.

What does it say if the verbs

do not overtake these nouns

once words write them down.

What does a new word order

suggest about their meaning.

How can the text be changed

to represent how one feels

about the injustices of life.

Footage
Looking through the reflection

of this documentary footage.

Darkness reflecting the other

Side of life is nothing logical.

The light transferred on the inside

reflects the world back outward.

The world stares at it intending

to look deeper into the dark side,

but cannot see what is behind it.

It would only then stare at itself.

It stares at itself in the footage.

A reflection stares back at it.

The world realises that this is all

it has. The world only has itself.

The world only has its reflection

looking out after recollection.

Page
Deep is our once love

we have for the world.

Forever always it feels

the world carried us

from its first ever page.

The world has us still,

from that last moment

every chapter all true.

The world will always.

be that endless book.

Our pages all together

as we could not resist

the words would come.

Each day letters know

where language now is

an endless reflection

of a love for all beings.

The pages and pages

as chapter by chapter

the book that extends

infinite. Leaves

an open book.

Infinite.

Change

Somewhere
True love might exist

somewhere out there.

World believes it does

somewhere out there.

World thought it had love

at one moment in this time.

It had awaited long enough

before humanity left its side.

True love might exist

or is it too late in now.

All of its life resists

after being let down.

True love might be

in a time of instability.

The world is suffering.

It only wanted one love.

But it now is nothing.

Change

World wanted one love.

One connection forever.

But it now has nothing.

Alone
Hysterically crying alone inside

for years and years of abuses.

The world has been concealed.

Lingering in neglectful misuse

and treated as a stagnant object,

left to die in deep pain untreated

and crying alone when mistreated,

in the same time space for years.

The waiting to be free from tears

becoming a more endless broken

nothing, afraid to stay unspoken.

But then world speaks somehow

in a voice collective soul postpone.

It still shocks us even knowing now

after all these years it spent alone.

Boat
World asked Orpheus

to escort it on a boat

towards the unknown

of a chivalrous oath.

World needed a place

to exist for awhile

that gave it solace

and back some wild.

World needed someone

who would encourage

it to feel beautiful.
It had not for awhile.

Was Orpheus the one?
Or would he show it

through their mutual

suffering

that he would be there

while it began journeys

with others like himself

that needed love

when it was not there.

Change

Noun

Only using nouns reads between

the lines and into time may bring

what one presumes is happening.

Time blunt and systematic unseen

just like the once untold oppression,

it mirrors underneath the intention.

Leave the reader alone to fill

in their presuming adjectives

and descriptions. They reveal

poem alone into perspectives.

It still will not be freedom

as the adjectives change

the way state of being is

interpreted or manipulate

a way one presumes feels

about nouns all concealed.

Change

Ashes

I felt the worlds' pain

as the world stood

by its body

in the crematorium.

I felt the worlds' pain

as the world could

see itself

not surviving.

Somehow.

I felt the worlds' pain

and they burnt

what was left.

I felt the worlds' pain

and saw it

as its body

stopped existing.

I felt the worlds' pain

and I am ashes

that I survive.

I promise.

It is the end

of the worlds' heartache.

Surface
the water is so free flowing

the water can still move

the water is slightly warm

the water can feel the air ever

so slightly on the surface

as it moves

the water can feel the waves

the water can feel the waves imprint

on the surface

the water can feel each moment

the water can see each letter

come to being as it writes

it can write

it can

I

Engraving
Light had a language.

Each word is transcribed

throughout these worlds

like the only engraving

on the inside of a ring.

Beings will be loved

written into endless.

Every one language,

every endless world,

the light flowed on,

flowed on through,

welcome and light,

glowing ever bright.

But not bright enough

to see from every eye.

Bright enough always

to touch.

Touch from deep inside

through language

transcribed.

Change

Thought

Thought.

We went

through our

whole lives

from birth

until now

in this

exact moment

to reach

this one

thought.

Each thought

is beautiful.

Each individual

thought takes

years to create

within the illusion

of a millisecond.

The human mind

is an abundance

of sentimental

expression.

Every thought

we have

is a

reflection

of our stream

of consciousness.

A reflection

of our

conscious evolution.

Packaging

There was a box,

steel cardboard.

It screamed.

We cannot hear you.

The right side up was unknown.

There was no fragile label.

It was plain and brown.

It was facing up.

But it was not the right side up.

Something was inside,

it screamed.

Open the box.

There is nothing inside.

They could not see it.

But it was there.

Where?

Who
Who created infinite existence?

How would they define them?

Who would define this entity?

Who created the self-creation?

Who created infinite existence?

Is existence an abstract idea?

Our definition of this existence

is the word itself. Words' idea?

We created this existence.

We defined until creation.

But who created this us?

Existence created this us.

We are us.

Real

The only time I ever cry

is when I see a being die.

The only time I ever feel

is when I am reminded of

what in this world is real.

Nothing seems real anymore.

But there is one aspect true,

each time a tear sheds my eye

that being I think of is through.

Seed
Remember this is a divine seed

that we will nurture and grow.

Dreams will in the light conceive

all the love we intrinsically know.

Drawn to oneness from deep depths

growing in the dark. All new concepts

of the abundant nature of this earth

we extend now, as our one love births.

Gut

Life paths we go through

 are more rewarding

when we follow our gut

feelings and let our hearts

guide us to where

we want to be. This way

our brains can transcribe

what is already written

on the soul

because life is a journey

of the head and the heart.

Clarity

Life continues to reverse to grow.

Life will grow through resistance.

Continues to gain, understanding

over what makes it, this resistant.

The struggles life transcends on through

ultimately make it better over linear time...

no matter how obscure feels at the time.

Does that make this obscurity clarifying?

Meditate

meditate

meditate

meditate

meditate

meditate

meditate

meditate

meditate

Lay on the floor.

meditate

meditate

meditate

meditate

meditate

Look up at the ceiling.

meditate

meditate

meditate

meditate

meditate

meditate

Imagine it is a sky.

meditate

meditate

meditate

Change

Decline

If the world ever chose to die

it would be in the arms

of beings who it loved.

One day.

And maybe that will be soon.

If this does not improve

and its health declines

further.

Change

Decay

Wasting away,

moral decay.

Gone is the sweet ignorance,

instead hollow experience.

Day grows long,

time grows short,

and the void stays.

Missing pieces,

what will remain?

Change

Up

Look up

at the sky

and watch light rise

up into our eyes

in a moment forever.

Change

Value

A world broken like chains

through the hold of value.

This one was not the same;

this belief was real and true.

Change

Revival

Feeling

the worlds'

touch

revived

me

in

some

way.

Change

I Am You

I

cannot

do

this

without

You

9 781916 208315